Elevation Above Status
"Inspirational poetry" Vol.1

Table Of Contents

Table Of Contents	1
Introduction	4
A Moment Can Last A Lifetime	7
The Words Of A Man	8
Finding That Perfect Someone For You	10
Faith And Belief Is Life's Relief	14
Your First Love Is Your Last	15
Limited Subscriptions And Restrictions	17
Exchanging Me For We	19
Love With False Utilization	20
The Qualities Of A Stranger	21
The Visualization Of A Fair Circumstance	22
The Man With No Definition	23
The Worst Thing Could Be The Best Thing	24
Forgive Them For All They Know	26

Elevation Above Status
"Inspirational poetry" Vol.1

A Man's Fight With The Devil	27
The Punishment For Love	29
The Love That Never Ends	31
Guidance For A Child	32
What Love Is	33
His Best Everything	34
Take Control Of Your Life	35
The Words Of A Women	36
Love Is Forever	38
Good And Bad Choices	39
The Reality Of Your Dreams	41
A Lost Of A Mother Is A Lost Like No Other	42
Who God Is	43
Falling In Love With My Pain	44
Who You Are	46
Living One Second To The Next	47
Underestimating The Underestimated	49

Elevation Above Status
"Inspirational poetry" Vol.1

How Much Of This Is Enough	50
Something Is Better Than Nothing	51
The Ending Is The Beginning	52
A Woman With No Definition	54
love Needs To Love	55
Frozen In Time	57
Living With Motivation	57
The New Year And The Old Year	59
Because It Was Those Times	60
Moments Like This You'll Always Miss	62
A Victim Of Wanting To Be Right	64
Lifes Journey	66
The Power Of Our Love	67
Little Things Are The Biggest	69
My Wife	70
Consideration For You	71
Broken Heart	72

 *Elevation Above Status*
"Inspirational poetry" Vol.1

Whats A Father	73
Whats A Mother	74
I'm Still Here	76

Introduction

This book has been created with the understanding of complications plaguing societies throughout the world. ***"Elevation Above Status"***, originated as a program, inducted by Variable Enhancement Services Non-profit community development organization, founded and developed in Brownsville, Brooklyn, New York in 1996.

After acknowledging many people being affected by the lack of education, employment, property and business owner rates, Variable Enhancement services began to be more involved with community issues and started assisting disadvantaged individuals and families throughout communities achieve a better life. Variable Enhancement Services soon started academic, vocational and spiritual

Elevation Above Status
"Inspirational poetry" Vol.1

education programs, designed to enhance their abilities to be aware and acquire environmental resources, opportunities, and understanding their adversities.

In 2009 the President of Variable Enhancement Services founded and wrote a program called Elevation Above Status, designated towards uplifting spirits and giving individuals a better outlook on life, while motivating their ability to make appropriate decisions pertaining to life's long accomplishments. In 2010 Derrick Pringle Sr. began to write what he knows to become inspirational elevations. These elevations soon became the handbook issued to program members who suddenly becoming very enlightened by the lessons learned.
In 2011 Derrick D Pringle Founded Pringle property services and began writing an extended version of the first

Elevation Above Status
"Inspirational poetry" Vol.1

handbook, called **"Elevation Above Status "Inspirations" Vol 1.** *(The book you are about to read)* influenced by the experiences and the spiritual revelations of its author, and the belief of inspiring and educating humanity. By reading Elevation Above Status "inspirations", The author is sure you will have a different outlook on life, a greater spiritual connection with your soul, receive multiple confirmations on previous life experience and in your everyday Activities.

A Moment Can Last A Lifetime

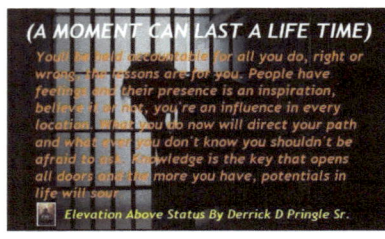 Words are weapons and could cut deeper than a sword, no matter the circumstances, they will never be ignored, be careful what you say because you can speak things into existence, when motivated by the demons of anger and frustration, you should fight their persistence. Mistakes are made when you're unaware of your actions, all others are choices that didn't meet your satisfaction. You can never take back the things you give and the marks they leave will remain as long as you live, you can change your future although you

Elevation Above Status
"Inspirational poetry" Vol.1

cannot change your past, and the memories created will always last.

You are held accountable for all you do, right or wrong, the lessons are for you. People have feelings and their presence is an inspiration, believe it or not, you're an influence in every location. What you do now will direct your path and whatever you don't know you shouldn't be afraid to ask. Knowledge is the key that opens all doors, and the more you have, potentials in life will sour.

He made the decision to go down that block, had he chosen a different route, he would have never gotten shot, he listened to his friends, believing they were telling the truth, had he known better, he would not be talking to his wife behind a glass and sitting in a booth. If only in those instances he would have made a different choice, His wife would not have teary eyes or a saddened voice. His kids wouldn't be alone, and he would be at home, now he's in the penitentiary fighting over the phone, up every day with stress on his mind, wishing it was over, and the minutes can rewind. He's facing a murder charge, and his courage has declined, acknowledging how a moment can last a lifetime.

The Words Of A Man

He sits in a room full of gloom, contemplating deeply on

Elevation Above Status
"Inspirational poetry" Vol.1

how to presume, his life is really rough and the struggle is getting tough, thinking about his family and how he could

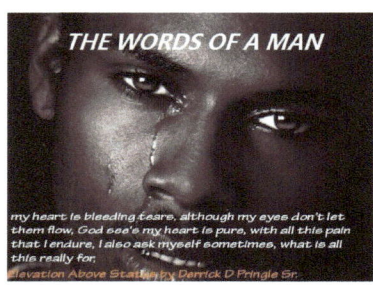

ever provide enough, finances are very low, his progress is moving slow, times are getting harder than people could ever know, his wife doesn't understand, he's trying to be all the man that he can, but chances are very slim, and it seems like there is no success in the world for him, he attempts to be discreet, although his spirit is getting weak, his wife enters the room and she begins to speak, " This doesn't make no sense and you need to get a job, on top of all that, you have been living like A slob, you don't clean up behind yourself, and you think you have a maid, this is not the 17th century and I'm definitely not a slave.

You're still not getting paid and the bills are stacking high, it seems as if with life you're afraid and you don't even try. I'm married to you, but I ask myself why, you're like a sorry excuse for a man and on my two feet only we stand. I take care of the house and kids all by myself and it's by the grace of God I can, as things get thick, you make me sick and the sight of you I can't stand". He looks for a moment with a sign of despair, trying to find the words, but all he

Elevation Above Status
"Inspirational poetry" Vol.1

can do is stare, his wife means the world to him and all he does is for her and his kids although he knows she doesn't understand how hard it is for him to live, accepting the rejection from all potential jobs, trying to break the cycle, although this deli-ma proceeds to revolve, nothing appears to be changing and there's nothing's given free, he hesitates for a moment but then he begins to speak," I love you honey, more than words can explain, your discrepancies bother me and I know it's not a game, I pray, wish And hope for my success, I've given this my all, and I'm doing my best.

I feel bad as a man and I'm doing all that I know, my heart is bleeding tears, although my eyes don't let them flow. God sees my heart is pure, with all this pain that I endure, I also say to myself sometimes, I do not need this, I need more. I see no appreciation, you're my wife with no relation, I'm tired of this sad song and I want to turn the station, this same old, sick band, playing this tune that I can't stand, what's even worse, my wife can't hear the words of a man.

Finding That Perfect Someone For You

I was speaking to a friend/confidant and said to them, "It is

Elevation Above Status
"Inspirational poetry" Vol.1

very difficult to find the one that's right for me", and they asked, "what type of person are you looking for?", and I responded, "A person that doesn't argue and wants to be happy always, a person that wants to keep negativity out of our relationship and understands the importance", they replied, " well it sounds like you're looking for a 100% person and they don't make those, in fact a perfect person doesn't exist because everyone is gonna have disagreements, this person sounds like a robot", I hesitated for a minute as I thought the last verse of the statement was a little sarcastic, knowing I should find the appropriate words to reply and not let that verse influence my response, I said, "You're right, there isn't a perfect person doesn't exist because everyone is gonna have disagreements, this person sounds like a robot".

I hesitated for a minute as I thought the last verse of the statement was a little sarcastic, knowing I should find the

Elevation Above Status
"Inspirational poetry" Vol.1

appropriate words to reply and not let that verse influence my response, I said, "You're right, there isn't a perfect person in the world for the world, although there is a perfect person in the world for me, I know people are gonna always have disagreements but disagreements are so minor and would never be a problem, it's easy to agree to disagree, they can like yellow and I can like blue, they can like rice and I can like potatoes, they can think the faster way home is different from the way I take, this is nothing to argue about because it is not that serious, in fact, it should be accepted as normal life, everyone is entitled to their own opinion, as that is all it would be", I heard a pause on the phone for a few seconds and then I heard them speak, " Well, I hear that, but you will still have arguments, because I know couples who've been together for 50 years and they go through it, so what will make you different from them?"

I smiled at the thought of my response and said, " I'm not different from them, although the outcome of my relationship can and will be different, let me explain".

# *Elevation Above Status*
"Inspirational poetry" Vol.1

"The reason couples argue is because they complain, saying, I want this and you did this and you did that and this is how it makes me feel, I deserve this and I deserve that and this makes me tired and yada yada yada". In response, the other one says, " well I do this because you did that and I feel like this because you didn't do that and I want this and you don't give it, I'm tired of this and I'm tired of that, yada yada yada". "the solution to this is very simple, this is not easy but I know we can practice, as I've come to find, both parties are selfish, instead of being selfless, each one of them are always on the defensive and wants to be understood, thinking the other doesn't understand them, but feeling they understand the other person, they need to try being the person who came into the relationship saying I love you, I'm concerned about you, I care about your feelings, but this is not what they're showing. To put it blunt, It should never be about you, you gave up I, you gave up me, when there became a we, now it's time for you to stop thinking about you and think about them and they need to do the same, check yourself and how

Elevation Above Status
"Inspirational poetry" Vol.1

you're making them feel and they'll do the same, this means, there will be no reason to worry about how they are making you feel because it is no longer your job, it's their job, it's your job to worry about how you're making them feel. Not saying you shouldn't be concerned about you, but trust and know they got you. Of course you will express your feelings and emotions, however, they won't come across as a complaint, only as a notification, because the tone of voice you use will flow with such easiness, knowing they are always taking you in consideration and it has been there vowed determination to do so, they are now selfless instead of selfish",

There was a moment that went by and my friend surprised me by saying, "I'm gonna be my own person and not walk in the shoes of my significant other and If you ever find that person please let me know, because I don't think it's possible." I paused on the phone in shock before responding and I said, "did you not hear anything I've said?, It's no longer about you, and if it is, that's all the reason to stay single, but anyway, you're entitled to your

Elevation Above Status
"Inspirational poetry" Vol.1

own opinion and I will let you know when I find that perfect someone for me, hoping that one day you'll began finding that perfect someone for you.

Faith And Belief Is Life's Relief

Before anything can be, at first there must be belief, driven by trust, faith delivers your life's relief. Words are spoken and actions are heard, your works produce facts with the

outcome you deserve, how can you prove to others what you can't prove to yourself, not finishing what you have, but yet looking for something else. Gambling on a feeling or a thought that holds no water, trying hard to avoid hell, while remaining close to the border. If you don't believe in something you might receive nothing, blinded by your own world, missing your blessings, because you never saw them coming.

Elevation Above Status
"Inspirational poetry" Vol.1

When you change your mind your life will follow, and your new decisions will reflect your tomorrow, because you decide to live right doesn't mean you'll see a total difference overnight. Any and all things take time to create and patients would prove to produce a prosperous fate. If you want different results you must do different things, everything will remain the same if your heart doesn't change, there is no one to blame but you, because you'll only receive results from what you choose. There is true everything for everyone, just when you think it's over, the best part has just begun. Remember all great things on earth are free and the only promise you have is to be deceased, cling to none of what you hear and half of what you see, always knowing faith and belief is life's relief.

Your First Love Is Your Last

I loved you when I was nothing and before I had something, even when I didn't understand life, you were

Elevation Above Status
"Inspirational poetry" Vol.1

destined to be my wife, life thrived for the understanding of the growth of my existence, leaving me in the darkness reminiscing on the future and what it held, although now the past speaks and I can see very well, I would only claim you, knowing what we have is forever true, if only then I knew, it was you, I would have not been affected by what we've been through.

You are the truth and the passion of my soul and the life we hold will continue to unfold, apart or together we will still remain, while acknowledging our loses and embracing our gains, I will never release, knowing you're my peace, I'll possess this passion until the day I'm deceased, Please remember me and the place we use to be, our love was priceless, yet we gave it to each other for free, no other love could ever compare, as our hearts distributed a love so rare, you are and will always be the best, all others will only be the rest.

Everyday I awake I'm reminded of where I am and just to make one step closer to you, I'll give it all that I can, you're

Elevation Above Status
"Inspirational poetry" Vol.1

my woman and I am your man, even if you don't have this in your plan, you could never fight love and you can't ever destroy fate, because wherever you decide to go, this is the starting place. My first, my last and evidently the beginning, the definition of "***The love that has no ending***", the love that keeps you thinking about the past, and keeps you reminded that your first love is your last.

Limited Subscriptions And Restrictions

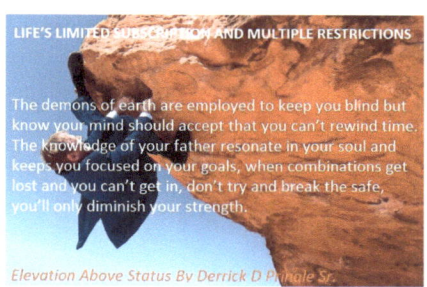

The limits of life will bind you to the restrictions of reality, although you submit your soul, you'll also become a casualty. No one is exempt from these promises by nature and your position will never become greater. The balance of the world will hinder the structure of your desire, never think you're better because you'll eventually feel the fire. Who are you to believe it can be a change without succumbing to pain, you're no different from the examples before you, as

Elevation Above Status
"Inspirational poetry" **Vol.1**

a matter of fact, the same things you'll go through.

No good deed goes UNpunished is what I say, and although you're righteous, you will also have to pay. Nothing good comes easy and graces are upon those who can relate, your power comes with a restriction and this is the ultimate fate. Acknowledge the soul of others and take heed to the mother, you will be challenged by your brother, as faith and belief prove to be like no other.

Don't change because another soul speaks; change because you can now blessedly see. The demons of earth are employed to keep you blind but know your mind should accept that you can't rewind time. The knowledge of your father resonates in your soul and keeps you focused on your goals, when combinations get lost and you can't get in, don't try and break the safe, you'll only diminish your strength. It's all up to you with only one direction to choose, and just like everyone, you don't have time to lose, but you will get bruised.No matter the circumstances or how much you give, life limits apply to all that live. This

Elevation Above Status
"Inspirational poetry" Vol.1

message is for those who listen, giving knowledge on life's limited subscription and multiple restrictions.

Exchanging Me For We

Combining yourself with your mate creates a new slate, all the past selfish methods of living you cannot take. This is a  new beginning with a person you want to see no ending, your life will completely change, pushing yourself in a world that's strange, there can only be one and it's the combination of the two, bringing the world together and all they've been through, changing your outlook on existence and distorting your facts, they're definitely coming with baggage you need to be willing, and helping unpack. This moment was meant for you, defining the reasons for all you knew, you're no longer by yourself and living as such compromises the relationships wealth. Everyone has a limit to which they could withstand, although this unity has no limit in the plan, you don't think

Elevation Above Status
"Inspirational poetry" Vol.1

about you, only think about us, always knowing unities longevity and survival is a must. Have the understanding in your heart, mind and soul you're never alone, and in their heart, mind and soul you are always at home. It's your place to uplift and give praise for their success, always wanting to see them prosper, knowing it's also you at your best, confidence is everything, in them you'll see a jewel, priceless being is a better notion, with love being the better fuel. You will understand the abundance of its demand, because it would be evident for your eyes to see, the time has come, with a passionate plea, for you to be exchanging me for we.

Love With False Utilization

Everything good is always taken advantage of and nothing gets an exception, not even Love, taking its kindness for its weakness, slandering its name in the street, becoming a victim of defamation and it's not you they appear to see, the residual of a passion so deep, not allowing reality to speak, your blinded by a moment so intense, wondering if this feeling could always commence, your mind is not focused on anything but the pain, you're dying inside, not wanting this emotion to remain, you desire change, although these thoughts are driving you insane, you're dwindling away

Elevation Above Status
"Inspirational poetry" Vol.1

from what's important, while life seems to be unfair, you're having crazy thoughts and not thinking very clear, why does the love hurt so bad? This is the question you will ask and it will always be around, love is suppose to pick you up and not let you down, you put all your faith in peace felt by

the essence of love's presence, only to be disappointed and forced into a lesson, tears don't heal, when you're done crying the feeling is still real, wishing it was a dream is all you seem to do, awakening to love's betrayal being evident and true. Everyone wants love, although love doesn't play it's part, it woe's you with a presence, gets comfortable and stabs you in the heart. This is not love, love only heals and helps grow, love is kind, patient and waiting for you if you're slow. You'll know it's not love, only people's representation and those who are betraying love with false utilization.

The Qualities Of A Stranger

Strangers are very underrated and don't get the credit deserved. A stranger can make you feel better than people who call themselves loving you; Strangers don't

Elevation Above Status
"Inspirational poetry" Vol.1

discriminate on who you are. Strangers don't judge you or dictate false information about you, because they don't know you. When meeting a stranger you have the

opportunity to present yourself as you are and not be looked on as changing or representing a false image, you can be yourself. Strangers don't have a conflict of interest in anything pertaining to you and will give you the best advice.

It seems as if a stranger can be a best friend to have, as long as they remain a stranger. When you want to get closer to them and like who they are, you now become subjected to disappointment and pain, which comes from people you are close to. It really sounds strange, but as you can see, strange can be good, so why not understand and give credit where it is due. The next time you meet a stranger, acknowledge the Qualities they have and know it's best sometimes for them to remain a stranger.

Elevation Above Status
"Inspirational poetry" Vol.1

The Visualization Of A Fair Circumstance

Most of the time when you meet someone, you're meeting their representative, the person they want you to believe they are. Most people are living for the acceptance of others, based on everything they do. When a person tells

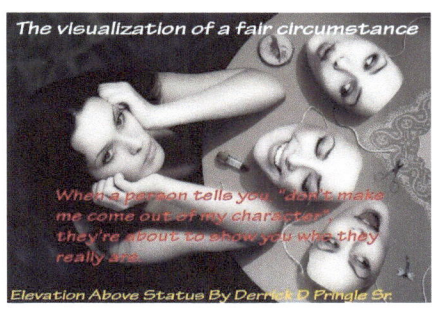

you, "don't make me come out of my character", they're about to show you who they really are. Why would anyone want to live in a character form? They

are either ashamed of their true being or their true being is widely disapproved of. This is manipulation and widely practiced by many, although, you can realize the genuineness of an individual when you notice them speaking in their own voice, responding in a unique manner and not in the manner in which they feel others would want to hear them. These characteristics of others are dangerous and found to be a physical and spiritual plague, you can

Elevation Above Status
"Inspirational poetry" Vol.1

help alter the process with your knowledge and integrity, giving you the visualization of a fair circumstance.

The Man With No Definition

The words he speaks are so unique, as he makes love to your mind with a verbal chemistry, it's like a melody that resonates deep within, piercing your soul and having you wonder how did this begin. "This man", you say, as your heart feels to get involved, although you feel that any moment this feeling can dissolve, but what you see appears to be different because your gut never lie, and it's either now or never, so you give this feeling a try, your heart is beating slowly as you creep towards the truth, knowing this man is unpredictable, you fathom his next move, Your thoughts are weary, although your spirit is content, you're convinced with the notion, this man was heaven sent. Your days are short and your nights are long, you attempt to humble yourself as the days carry on, you cringe on every sight, his morals appear so right. You ask yourself, "Could

Elevation Above Status
"Inspirational poetry" Vol.1

this be my fate?", "Is this why God had me wait?","Is this the answer to my dreams or the nights I kneeled and prayed"?

This man is so attractive, mentally, spiritually and on a physical stage, imagine him being in a picture in a book and you're not wanting to turn the page. This man seems pure, confident, respected by most and met with no opposition, this man is rare, righteous, thoughtful and kind, it's hard to give a description, this man distributes peace, love, and the embodiment of harmony, like filling your medical prescription, his essence is free, for the world to see, this is the man with no definition.

Elevation Above Status
"Inspirational poetry" Vol.1

The Worst Thing Could Be The Best Thing

Sometimes your life has to be turned upside down in order for you to live right side up, having you think to yourself, saying "enough is enough", your days will get dim and your nights will get cold, you'll be at the bottom with only one way to go, that's up, you'll finally see your fate, with the acknowledgement of your destiny and your following

Elevation Above Status
"Inspirational poetry" **Vol.1**

not being too late. Your mind is clear and you'll see no such thing as a friend, and only true love you receive will see you through to the end.

There can not be construction without demolition and finally, in your life, you'll know what's been missing, self respect, self love and self worth, you wont need a doctor, nor will you need a nurse. All you'll need is faith, understanding and belief, giving thanks to the father for your spiritual relief.

Things are different now and your days are not wasted, and with love, righteousness, concern and purity, you are able to face it, nothing in life will ever be the same, because you've accepted your failures and know it was only you to blame, forgiveness is freedom and you will never be a slave, living your life in God's eyes and respecting what he's made, with understanding, truth, trust and sincerity, the wisdom you now possess will give you clarity, you'll look back on the pain and destruction with the blessing of change, seeing God in everything, in Jesus name,

Elevation Above Status
"Inspirational poetry" Vol.1

embracing the joy, in which the future may bring, knowing the worst thing that can happen can often be the best thing.

Forgive Them For All They Know

When you're hurting and not understanding why your child calls another person mommy or daddy, because you were never around, forgive them, for that's all they know. When you're hurting and wanting to obtain a better relationship with your parents, but always get disappointed with their actions, based on their upbringing and their internal issues, Forgive them, for that's all they know.

When you're dealing with an abusive relationship and your significant other abuses alcohol or drugs, because of his or her abusive childhood, forgive them, for that's all they know. When you're in a relationship and you're dealing with the jealousies and insecurities of your significant other, based on their previous experiences with bad relationships, forgive them, for that's all they know. When you are angered by the deception, defamation, and the name slandering of certain individuals, knowing they've been raised in a disrespectful environment with no self-value, forgive them, for that's all they know.

When you're dealing with a loved one who can't or doesn't want to get a job and they have always been in the street chasing dead end dreams, forgive them, for that's all they know. When you look at television and see all the government corruption, prejudiced activities, injustices , and the deception of the people, because it's been inducted into the way of life since the country has been created, forgive them, for that's all they know. When it appears that the whole world is against you, they are really against themselves; as long as you're righteous you'll prevail , because when you know better you'll do better, so always forgive them for all they know..

Elevation Above Status
"Inspirational poetry" Vol.1

A Man's Fight With The Devil

 Your soul begins to hemorrhage from the blows filled with death, your eyes fluttering with anguish as you gasp for breath. Your mind speaks loudly in a fainting voice and the words you hear deliver your final choice. "I will not quit, I'm stronger than this, although I'm weak and can barely ball a fist". My spirit is tough and I know I had enough; But the Devil is a liar and I'm going to call his bluff". I've been hurt before, I'm no stranger to pain; In fact, my pain encouraged me to change. I re-positioned my approach and reconditioned what I wrote, reevaluated my style and turned my frown into a smile. As I showed this, the devil poked me in the eyes, blinding my site and taking me by surprise. He knocked me off my feet and had me down on the ground, then whispered to me with a deep harsh sound. "I will show you who I am, and you will for fill my plan, no matter what you do; you can't flee from me, I can only flee from you, I

Elevation Above Status
"Inspirational poetry" Vol.1

will always have my way, doing as I see fit and choose, this is my planet earth, the place I call home and for long as you live here, I'll never leave you alone". I then moved my head around as I lay on the ground, although I thought death was imminent, I no longer heard a sound. I began to look to God, asking him, ``Why you have forsaken me; suddenly I heard a voice as my eyes began to see." This is for you my son, your life has just begun, you no longer have to hide and you no longer need to run, they say the devil is a liar, but his lies you turned to truths, because all he expect of you is exactly what you do, when times get rough you took none of the blame, but what you give is what you get and as it went is how it came. This is your lesson as well as your blessing; there is no time for wondering and no time for guessing. Take this, because it's yours, you were there when it began and you are the reason for the cause. There is no one to blame, but you, and that's true, so don't point the finger, just do what you need to do." After hearing from God, everything became level and I realized this was normal, just a man's fight with the devil.

Elevation Above Status
"Inspirational poetry" Vol.1

The Punishment For Love

How can something so right turn out to be so wrong? How can something that feels so good end up hurting so bad? Love is a blessing, but it can sometimes feel like a punishment. When a person gives their heart to anything, they give their soul and anyone on the other end should acknowledge the gift... love is a great thing and to be able to say you've experienced it is very special and unique. Some people take this wonderful blessing for granted and make the person who loves them feel as if they are wrong for doing so, because with every look and response to all of the attention they are given, it appears as if they don't desire it. it really doesn't make any sense when everyone wants love, why should anyone feel as if they are being punished for loving...they want to be with you all the time, they call you and talk to

Elevation Above Status
"Inspirational poetry" Vol.1

you hours at a time, all they ever do is think of you and want to provide you with all that you need and desire, their life feels empty without you, this is all good things and the feeling that should result in this should be good.

Your heart should be open to receive love, just as you would want another person's heart open to receive love from you. Your arms and heart should always embrace the comfort of the love that's being given to you, a person should love and not appear to hate love. If someone wants to love you let them, why punish them, because love doesn't hurt you intentionally. Someone who cares for you and loves you is giving you a reward; they shouldn't receive a punishment in return.

The Love That Never Ends

It's the love that never ends, it's the love you can't help but share with your friends, it's the love that pumps your blood, the love that you'll call love, the one you're always thinking of, it's the love that shines so bright and keeps you up at night, it's the love you can't resist and many times you reminisce, it's the love that hurts the most and the reason

Elevation Above Status
"Inspirational poetry" Vol.1

you kept them close, It's the love you can't forget, when you thought they were heaven sent, and the love you so  proclaim, hoping for the day you carry the name, it's the love you'll do all for and the moments you so adore, your mind will forever be there and your soul will forever care, the reason you do your hair and the feeling you get when they're there. It's the love that sets you free and takes you where you want to be, it's a love that has no fear and only wants you here, it's the love you won't erase and know nothing could take its place, wishing the love was bound and nothing could keep it down, It's the love that keeps you going, and in your heart you are forever knowing, it's the love that makes you insane, saying to the person, "you need to stop playing", this love might not be a wanted trend, but it's the love that never ends.

Elevation Above Status
"Inspirational poetry" Vol.1

Guidance For A Child

After the first decade of a child's life, they begin to question the parent's judgment and often can become rebellious. A parent must take in consideration of the child's feelings, because a child begins to feel emotionally neglected. For all their lives, their parents have dictated what they should do or should not do, and with no exception. However, a child consciously begins to realize, no one is always right.

A parent must take the approach of consoling the child's emotions, because their children's influences don't only come from them. Everyday, like it or not, a child is exposed to all ways of life and all conditions and a parent must not take that for granted. A parent should begin by explaining their

Elevation Above Status
"Inspirational poetry" Vol.1

acceptance of not being perfect and their decisions aren't always the correct one, but also explaining how their intentions are towards the child's best outcome.

Everyone gives respect, when another person acknowledges their own imperfection and they also respect the emotional understanding they receive. This would often have the child to not rebel and would have them respect the parent's dictation, knowing it is only for their future and the best guidance for a child.

What Love Is

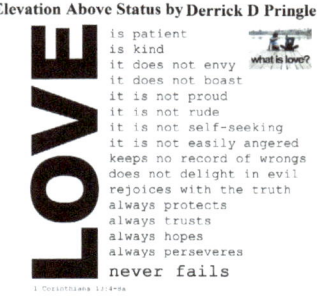

Love is calling you up just to let you know it's there, Love is thinking of you all the time, Love is considering you first, love is praying for you always, Love is concerned about your feelings, Love is wanting to see you smile, Love is patient, Love is Kind and caring, Love is missing you when you're not around for only a minute, Love is complimenting you, love is admiring you, Love is waiting up for you at night, Love is loving you through

Elevation Above Status
"Inspirational poetry" Vol.1

your wrongs, love is forgiving you always, love is encouraging you to do better, love is standing by your side through ups and downs and for better or worse.

Love is protecting you from all harm, verbally, emotionally or physically. Love is the power that makes you feel wanted and needed. Love is helping you in your time of need, love adores every little thing about you, your walk, talk and the little funny things you do, and love is always speaking highly of you. Love is your friend, partner, confidant and companion. Love is a blessing from God, Love is one of God's greatest gifts, Love is what God has for the world as he gave his only son. Love is inspiration, Love is healing, Love is power, Love is faith, Love is hope, Love is unbeatable, Love is invincible, Love is everlasting, Love is Forever, Nothing can buy it and nothing can take it, Wherever you find beauty, grace, harmony, joy, peace and no pain, Love Is..

His Best Everything

When a man finds a wife he finds a part of himself, although it's a great thing and will always be his life. She should receive anything and become his

Elevation Above Status
"Inspirational poetry" Vol.1

best everything. His best breath, His best thought, His best moments, His best smile, His best emotion, His best love, his best prayer, His best answer, His best dream, His best lesson, His best teacher, His best plan, His best friend, His best touch, His best kiss, his best hug, His best heartbeat, His best smell, His best gift, His best strength, His best home, His best vision and she shall receive the best of him, because she is his best everything, his wife.

Take Control Of Your Life

Many things are left better unsaid, although the temptation burns at your soul to release the words and let them flow. Revealing your feelings can do more damage than providing relief, and you need to be careful of the words

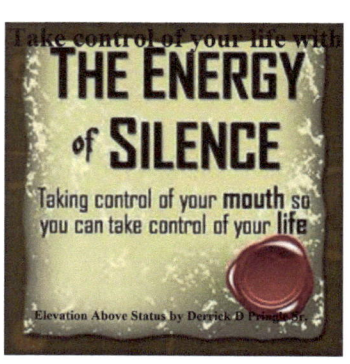

you speak. We all know that your actions speak louder than words, so by living your thoughts and emotions you would always be heard.

"Where does the power reside in silence?", is what you ask yourself. All words come from the emotions of how you're

Elevation Above Status
"Inspirational poetry" Vol.1

feeling or feel about someone or something. When revealing these emotions you're opening a door to your soul and inner being. What you must understand is, some emotions come from anxiety and fear of what you don't know and if you speak on them too soon, you can often be wrong, although having verbal silence, your body language can also speak volumes, so this also, you must control.

Your weakness and vulnerability resides in the words you speak and the body language you display, allowing people to see right through you, this gives them the power and control over your life, feeding you the words and penetrating your emotions, which will evidently influence your actions or reaction, making you their slave. Living like this can never be right, so hear these words today Saying, "Take control of your life".

The Words Of A Woman

The Words of a woman comes from the depths of her soul, as she speaks to her man asking him, "please don't go", he hears her, although he really doesn't listen, absorbing all the

Elevation Above Status
"Inspirational poetry" Vol.1

words but not realizing what he's missing. He says, "honey I got this and everything is going to be alright, I know you get lonely when I'm out all night, I'm working on our future , I'm getting things all together, my only plan is for us to do better."

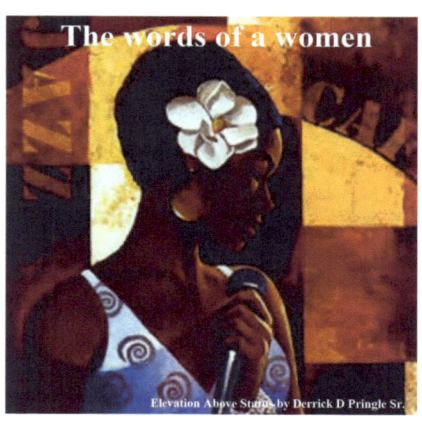 She stares at him with her sad and passionate eyes, as the cuticle waters swell up and she begins to cry, she thinks to herself as she looks deep into his soul, praying inside that God convince him not to go, feeling overwhelmed with an emotion oh so deep, clinging on to him as she weeps and begin to speak, "baby I know you got us and this I can't deny, but I also can't restrain from wondering the reasons why, please listen to me because my heart is getting weak, when you're gone at all times of night I can't rest or barely sleep, I need to be by your side

Elevation Above Status
"Inspirational poetry" Vol.1

because I see what you need to defeat, I'm more than your friend, your lover and your wife, I'm more than a woman that stays home when you leave for all times of the night, I'm your grace, your blessing and I'm your secret weapon, I hate when you walk out the door and keep it steppin.

He looks at her with a little frustration but also sympathize, because he can't help but see the sincerity in her eyes, wanting to stay in every way, but he knows what he needs to do, deep down in his heart and mind he knows what she's saying is true, he removes her arms and turns away and begin heading for the door, as he turns the knob and look back at her saying, "honey I don't want to discuss this anymore".

He has a night on the town and has to make his rounds and she don't know he's deep in the street, his mind is gone but he keeps moving on to a meeting that's waiting for him, he's striking a deal with a man that's for real and believe this one would be the last. He doesn't know that the Feds are gonna show and tonight it would be his ass. The lights

Elevation Above Status
"Inspirational poetry" Vol.1

come on and his friends are all gone while he thinks to himself in a cell, saying, "damn this is just not right, I was stupid, I was blind and I should have listened to my wife last night". Now she is done but her love won't let her run and she stays right by his side, because she's a woman a really good women, made to be down to ride, but deep inside it's hard to hide the fact she had never been heard, and every time she looks at him now she says, "damn, you should have listened to my words".

Love Is Forever

The fire burning inside of any individual is only the

symbolization of the devil's presence and all activity based on that fire will further destroy them. When you function on the anger and hate from the frustration inside of you, it will only define you. Don't become what makes you angry and fuel the fire that burns inside of you. You must extinguish this fire with the water of love and forgiveness. Why would you do the same thing to anyone which someone has done to you, hurting you so bad. You deemed this conduct to be terrible and evil. You hurt with a passion rarely known by many, but when getting a chance, you think to make the decision of becoming what you hate, by taking revenge. Take heed to these words and love and love more. When a fire is started and you attempt to extinguish it with the water of love to know avail, just leave and get far away, because God will put the fire out, the fire will eventually die, but love is forever.

Good And Bad Choices

What you want might come with a hidden price of a value greater than money, called time. In due time things become revealed, twice the size of its original image, more disturbing, you never see the picture clearly, until it's fully developed. How could you make these choices to move in this empty direction when it appeared to be so full? Was it your imagination, or was it your expectations? Either way,

Elevation Above Status
"Inspirational poetry" Vol.1

neither of those are appropriate when making choices which will guide your life. Face reality, you don't want things to spiral out of control so you work on what you've created, with hopes of making it better.

Time has no patience, and will go on without you. Eventually you will see this cycle repeat itself one time too many, but when would eventually come, and with what price. You are responsible for it all and should know when to realize when it's enough, but you're blinded by the first image, which wasn't fully developed and now you're trying to alter its exposure, but you can't. This picture is already made. All that remains is the direction you set off on, the mission of keeping your initial focus intact, but it's not for you to do. If something was in your power to control, you would need not apply force, it would flow naturally.

Your life can only receive what it is fed, just like a baby you live everyday gaining knowledge and getting stronger

Elevation Above Status
"Inspirational poetry" Vol.1

by accepting your bad choices and confirming it to be just that and nothing else. Many have problems with accepting fault or doing wrong, because of fear and degradation, but actually accepting your faults and bad choices is the opposite, it's your power, your strength to defeat what has risen against you from what you believed to be for you. Use your power and mold your future in the right direction, making everything better for sure. Neglect the words of others containing the seeds of damnation and move forward. remember the bad past for the energy of your strength and make choices to impact a bright future.

The Reality Of Your Dreams

Everyone wants to live a dream, although dreams can become a nightmare, your heart plays a big part, forever wanting you there, some people ask; "what's wrong with wanting a dream, when happiness is what dreams bring". A dream is not always what they seem and the promises they might not bring. Life takes you on a mental ride to the extremities of all its existence, keeping you wanting more and more, only to receive resistance. Giving love appears to

Elevation Above Status
"Inspirational poetry" Vol.1

be the way until you realize love only loves love and for loving you shall pay. Pain is no-longer pain and hurt is no-longer hurt; the only thing that's real is the thing that's going to work, righteousness, faithfulness and the ability to move on, because the same thing that's happening now will be happening after you're gone. You try to escape to the life of a dream, in-order to condition your heart, only to awake and still be in the dark. Now you can't see, and what you have left is what you cling to, because now you have awakened to the reality of your dreams.

A Lost Of A Mother Is A Lost Like No Other

O dear Mother, how I love you so much, and all I can remember is your loving touch, the days when I was weak you helped me win,

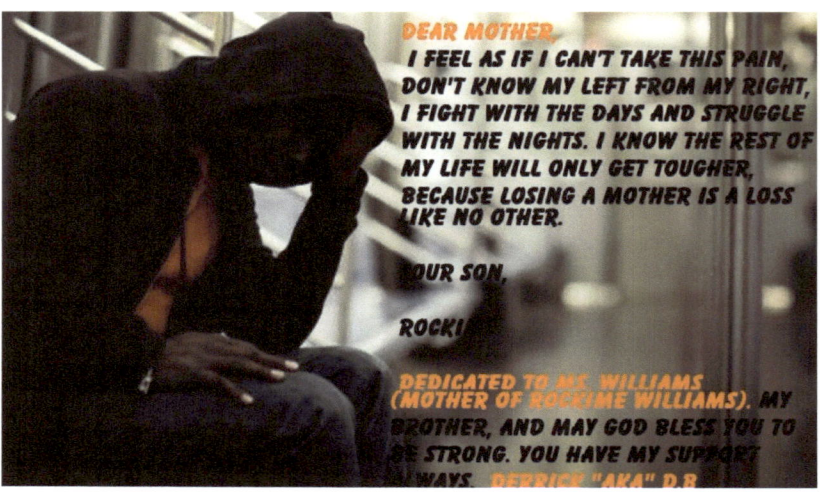

staying by my side through thick and thin. For all my days and even after I'm gone, I'll keep your memory alive as I've done since I was born. My pain is deep Ma', because you're not here with me, and it keeps hurting, that I cry so much, I can barely see. I'll try my best to hold out my chest, and move life forward knowing I'm blessed. I will compare women of my choice, as I've known you to be, giving love, assistance and respect, because it's totally free. You have a heart that heals all wounds, and I deeply feel that you were taken too soon. The pain in my heart will ache for a while, now I know what it's like for a mother to lose a child. Someone who cherishes you and their mind, body and soul is your home, leaving you to never imagine you'll ever be alone. There are people who love and care about me; but none like my mother who adores and cherishes the air I breathe. I feel as if I can't take this pain, I don't know my left from my right, I fight with the days and struggle with the nights. I know the rest of my life will only get tougher, because losing a Mother is a loss like no other.

Who God Is

God is love and love is god. God is waking up and telling your family you love them. God is comforting and caring. God is forgiving when you don't want to

Elevation Above Status
"Inspirational poetry" Vol.1

forgive. God is smiling when you don't want to smile. God is laughing when you don't want to laugh. God is thoughtful when no one else thinks about you. God is protecting when you feel UNprotected. God is telling you how beautiful you are, no matter what anyone says. God is helping you when you need a hand. God is providing shelter when you need a rest. God is giving you strength when you feel weak. God is complimenting you when you achieve. God is informing you it will be ok. God is understanding of all your concerns. God is telling you that you are special. God is walking with you through all your travels. God is seeing what you can't see. God is wisdom and knowledge. God is informing you of potential danger. God is in you if you are all of these things to others. God is Blessing you. God is.....so much more!

Falling In Love With My Pain

I feel like crying but the tears won't flow, although the pain from reality I can't let go I try and try to do better in life, but this pain I feel is just not right, I hold on to my faith and attempt to remain strong, although I don't know how long I

Elevation Above Status
"Inspirational poetry" Vol.1

can keep going on, I'm very offended and just want to end it, as my heart is so torn trying to find something to mend it. There has to be a better way of living day to day, because it seems as if nothing is going my way. But I must

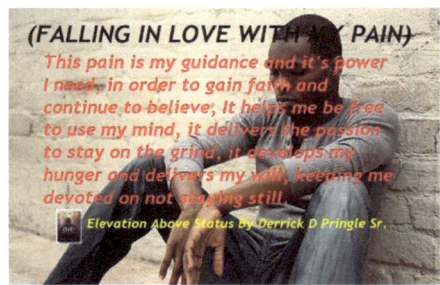

now stop and listen to the signs I've been missing, because I've been overwhelmed by the pain that has me near submission.

This pain is my guidance and it's power I need, in order to gain faith and continue to believe, It helps me be free to use my mind, it delivers the passion to stay on the grind, it develops my hunger and delivers my will, keeping me devoted on not staying still, it releases my stress, while keeping me at my best, I understand now the strategy of chess, It's not stress in fact it lets me know I'm blessed, and whatever doesn't kill me is only a test, I must endure this position and understand it's method, know its motivation, while keeping my soul protected, this is my power and its protege I must

Elevation Above Status
"Inspirational poetry" Vol.1

devour. At the same time I can't help but look for change, although this may seem strange, in order to beat this I must fall in love with my pain.

Who You Are

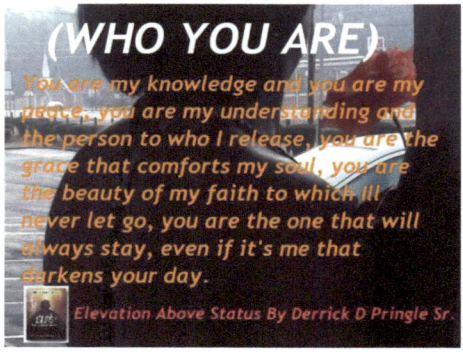

You are the reason I do all I do. You are the answer and the solution to the pain that always brewed. You are the evidence that love exists and you are the sight and reality I've always missed. You are who I think of in my dreams and you are the reality that differs from what things might seem, you are the answers to my prayers and you are God's way of showing me he cares, you are my wisdom, my friend, you are the person I need to see at the end, you are all I didn't believe, and you are a privilege like the air I breathe. You are my knowledge and you are my peace, you are my understanding and the person to whom I release,

Elevation Above Status
"Inspirational poetry" Vol.1

you are the grace that comforts my soul, you are the beauty of my faith to which I'll never let go, you are the one that will always stay, even if it's me that darkens your day, you are the light that shines my path and you are the addition in my life's mass, you are my hope and part of my praise, you are so elegant in so many ways, you are the truth when the demons attack, and when I'm in trouble you are the one that has my back, you are my sacrifice and the person for whom I'll give my life, you are a value that has no price.

You are unique, like the words I speak, you are the change that I am now, the opposite of what I use to be, you are my confidence and the choice for me to be better, you are the warmth I receive in the winter, you are my sweater, you are special and that's a fact by far, you are the twinkle in my life and yes you are my star, you are bigger than my plans, like a lawyer passing the bar, you are worthy of all that's pure, that's who you are.

Living One Second To The Next

They try to keep you down and when you make mistakes

Elevation Above Status
"Inspirational poetry" Vol.1

it's brought to your attention, like you were never there, like you're not aware. This is nature and made to be a fact of the people judging you, although it's not true, they will never know or have the feeling of what you've been through.

The body you inherit is for you to absorb the merit, but this is not what you want. Your mind craves more and better, while feeling like a feather, they attempt to discredit you, but you're the best and the life you live is much different from the rest. It's only for the moment and it will not exist unless you own it.

The time is now and the sound is loud among the crowd but God is your answer although the people produce cancer, while trying to spread poison. Who are you? What makes you better? Your sight sees beyond the image of deception, although the distraction is your weapon, you must realize the lesson.

It's not easy to see the elements designated to crush your progression, they hate you and this is sad but true. The first

Elevation Above Status
"Inspirational poetry" Vol.1

time you see the light of grace you replace the face of what means all to you and all you do, your reminder is the reality of the life you really live and the righteousness you always give. This might be now, as all this shall pass, not being different from the last, the best of the future is to what you grasp, because all you go through is nothing but a test, so with this challenge and many others you give your best, move on and treat all like the rest, while living one second to the next.

Underestimating The Underestimated

Sounds vague, maybe even hard to believe, although it's the silence that sounds louder, a chance at real love you feel the need to achieve, you give it your all, because your eyes live in your heart and through this organ you see, knowing the good you're giving others and it's what your expecting to receive, but the world doesn't make sense and doesn't take responsibility, you're plagued with defense and passing the blame is an easy ability. Nothing good comes easy, because easy comes and easy go's, you'll need to stay firm through the highs and the lows, respect the unexpected, in fact it is

Elevation Above Status
"Inspirational poetry" Vol.1

expected, not knowing these facts are like living life naked. Never neglect the power you possess, your weaknesses are your strengths and when you're down you're at your best. Your senses become stronger and your striving nevertheless, consciousness to the world will assist in eliminating stress. Everyone plays the fool sometimes and even gets humiliated, you'll say to yourself, "They have some nerve", because your intelligence they've degraded, It's been so long but you still move on, although the time you feel has been wasted, this is a lesson we all will learn when underestimating the underestimated.

How Much Of This Is Enough

You're putting your heart on the table, while keeping your soul on track, always looking forward, while your spirit is under attack, the days seem short and the nights appear endless, your prayers ask God will he ever end this. I'm blinded and can barely see, feeling like I don't want to continue being me, the life I'm living is the best I know how, wondering where I would be, if I knew before, what I know now. This pain is real, although, to hurt I'm no

Elevation Above Status
"Inspirational poetry" Vol.1

stranger, I wish this on no soul, as I feel so much anger, I'm a righteous soul and I feel so alone, vulnerable like a child, although fully grown, thinking about others and all they have to endure, cherishing the little things in life and being grateful to be poor, the more you have is the most you have to lose, finding yourself in a position with a difficult choice to choose.

No One is exempt, as we are all the same, praying to God and pleading for a change, we need to see the light as the roads are getting rough, our faith is being challenged, as living is getting tough, the damage is definitely done, although we have given our trust, while asking ourselves, how much of this is enough.

Something Is Better Than Nothing

I complain, I wish sometimes would disappear, but in all reality, I need to be grateful for the blessing of them being here, this is hard and this is strange, although I feel like it's not good for me, I'm afraid of change. Most of the time, I'm feeling all alone, a bottle or a substance I call home, I'm bigger than what I believe, and my sight is further than

Elevation Above Status
"Inspirational poetry" Vol.1

what I can see, there is a weight holding me down and all I want to do is grieve. It seems everything is gone, it's hard to move on, and I can't stop blaming myself for all that went wrong. Where is my God? This is all I need to know, the presence of him would help me grow, I feel no cure, although my heart is pure, this dilemma and pain is something I must endure. My life is righteous and my future is bright and with this knowledge I embrace the will to fight. I feel they all hate me, although this is not true, I should be grateful for the challenges I've been through.

I'm better now and my souls at peace, because I've learned about the pain and what I need to release, It's the memories that have me cry, it's the memories to which I don't want to say goodbye, It's the memories that attempt to kills my dreams, although I should know everything is never what they appear or seem. I know my strength and I follow my passions, I'll stay strong, no matter what

Elevation Above Status
"Inspirational poetry" Vol.1

happens. I can't be defeated because my God is cunning, although the worst will never stop coming, I'll stay put, from my fears I'll stop running, because if I didn't know then, I know now, something is better than nothing.

The Ending Is The Beginning

After it's all said and done, some say it's over, but you should know it's just begun. For many years you've ran and on your own, you stood, wondering to yourself if you ever could, there's never been a moment like this, as you feel totally different about what you thought you missed, your plan is yours and other plans are not the same, as for other people's mistakes you made yourself to blame, it's humility, yes in deed, accomplishing your goals and all you believe, these times are tough and many times you've been deceived, many lives have been lost and many times you've grieved, the tears are never ending and the sorrow seems to forever remain, holding on to the memories, while attempting to embrace the change. You're at a crossroad in your life, wondering how to keep your sense, feeling distorted by the signs of peace, because as they came, they

Elevation Above Status
"Inspirational poetry" Vol.1

went. This is the time when you need to be at your best and these are the times that's more vital than the rest. These are the times when you're forever so weak and the times when you can barely sleep, your heart seems faint with a slow beat, pain bothers you with silence, while the nights you try to defeat it. All of this makes you feel as if you're losing instead of winning, striving to remain righteous and refrain from sinning. Your words are going unheard and your cries are not convincing. Most of all, you're trying to understand what you're going through, not knowing the ending is the beginning.

A Woman With No Definition

She is not ordinary and she is not typical, she appears in abundance, although she's very simple, the finer things in life don't make her move, and in any situation wisdom is what she proves. She has self confidence, although she respects her man, as when devoted to any situation she gives all that she can. She believes she's never understood, and although embodied with good, her heart leads her places, her mind never could. She is adorable, and the word beautiful couldn't really compare, as she's thoughtful, kind,

Elevation Above Status
"Inspirational poetry" Vol.1

loving and the epidermal of care.

You can't help but love this woman because she's a lady first, similar to light and oxygen even when she's at her worst, she's stronger than strong, because the worst she has endured, you can't just have a part of her, you'll always desire more, she prays to God, asking for patients, understanding and the acceptance of submission, but the most she'll ever appreciate is for her husband to sit and listen, she's literally the best of the best and not just in the kitchen, It's complicated to give you a description of a woman with no definition.

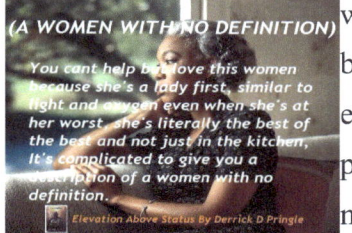

love Needs To Love

When your mind tells you no, although your heart tells you yes, you sit and contemplate on how to remain your best. Your chest ache from the internal pain that you feel, while asking yourself if this feeling could even be real, you're in an emotionally distorted place where there seems to be no

Elevation Above Status
"Inspirational poetry" Vol.1

return, while criticizing yourself, by saying, "will I ever learn, I seem to go down this same road after years of frustration, while being warned and told, I know it's bad for me, but I refuse to let go". After a while, your heartbeat doesn't even sound the same, you're feeling like a toy, because love keeps playing these crazy games. You would fix this if you could, but what should be the difference if love never understood. It's like you're damned if you do and you're damned if you don't, but at this point you'll do anything and there is nothing you won't.

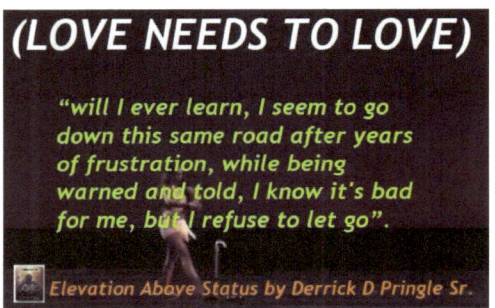

Tears don't help, as a matter of fact you're dehydrated, your soul is getting weak and about now you can't take it, you ask your lord to have mercy but it appears you're not being heard, promising to do right and reconditioning your word, pleading with a cry asking why does this exist, knowing you wasn't totally right, but there must have been

Elevation Above Status
"Inspirational poetry" Vol.1

something you've missed. All you really want is for things to get back to the way they were, living days in the essence of peace is what you're thinking of, it's time to release like a spark blowing the bulb, because love is the best thing in life, therefore love needs to love.

Frozen In Time

you can remember but you can't rewind, moments so rare that've been left behind. Constant memories of what you've been through, thinking about now and what if then you knew. Growing up is vital to life, but if it wasn't for then you couldn't get it right. Your decisions now have a whole lot of relation to what took place from that very location. Your dreams are built from what used to be, this is applied to you and me. I'll always be stern from everything I learned, from that time to the time I'm adjourned. It might have been rough and rocky along the line, but I'm motivated by those moments frozen in time

Living With Motivation

Being in a place of determination will allow you to

Elevation Above Status
"Inspirational poetry" Vol.1

complete your goals and not allow the deterrence of the demons to pro-vale. Unlike the blessings from God, the deterrence from the demons will attempt to cloud your sense of thought and throw you off balance. Your mind is stronger than you recognize and giving yourself credit should project you to extremely hold on to your initial determination.

There are plenty of negative spirits infecting souls around you and most of them don't have the power to help, guide, protect, understand or can even remove themselves from themselves and sooner or later they will find themselves by themselves, exposing them for who they are. These individuals will try and make you feel as if you're the problem, because your actions don't comply with their preferences or expectations.

Your greatest reward will be given through the sacrifice of yourself, your desires, your preferences and your reason to believe someone else is the problem, when the problem as well as the solution resides in you. It's common to pass the

Elevation Above Status
"Inspirational poetry" Vol.1

blame, it's common to look away from yourself and point the finger at others, because it's common to possess the desire to be right, although everyone is right, saying someone else is wrong, is wrong.

There will be many times where you'll find yourself in the midst of potential confusion and the elements around you will not be too encouraging towards looking at the positive examples of life and the passing perfections of problems. Sometimes you can only count on yourself and never forget to give what you have to others and only judge yourself and always love to demonstrate by living with motivation.

The New Year And The Old Year

Some marks or scars are easier to heal than others and most times they can't be replaced overnight or smothered, as you make new year's resolutions, it doesn't necessarily give you a solution, some new year's resolutions can also be a mental pollution, time is not defined in a eve of an attempted new beginning, although times definition comes after an old ending, the most productive interpretation should be combined with the continuation of winning. Bringing in the

Elevation Above Status
"Inspirational poetry" Vol.1

new year is a great concept, although the new year is composed of the last, it will help you positively understand your past. As many people take for granted the reality of new, it is only the embodiment of all you've been through. Even though your mind and spiritual process have changed, the mark you've left from your previous activities are still the blame. A repetitive cycle of an unwanted circumstance should leave you in a position to take a necessary glance, your life can't be right, if every year it appears you'll need to turn on a spiritual light. Reevaluating lessons will provide your ultimate blessing, leaving you in a place warranting your final correction, while having the challenge of an intermediate testing. Leave your past behind, also recognizing it's the reason you are here, the next level is just a higher number and you'll need to see it very clear. The future is now and remember time moves fast, knowing that every day can evidently be your last, the cycle might change but the rhythms are hard to tame, because this new year and the old year is the same.

Elevation Above Status
"Inspirational poetry" Vol.1

Because It Was Those Times

It was those times I needed you the most, you were like a ghost, it was those times I needed to hear a word, you chose not to be heard, it was those times my spirit longed for a touch from only you, the times I struggled hard with the thoughts you never knew, it was those times I needed to know you cared, you let them pass without a glare, you reeled me in with the compassion and love then made me feel like I would've been better off where I was, it was those times I cried and only you could stop my tears, although it was you who created my greatest fears. It was those times you spent with me, times I thought you were heaven sent and is meant to be, it was those times I waited for your call or even a text would have done fine, sending me your love, because you already had mine. It was those times we shared on those wonderful days, I believed in us, thinking they'll never change. It's those times I would've loved to rewind and erase these times I'm trying to get off my mind.

Elevation Above Status
"Inspirational poetry" **Vol.1**

It was those times love had me blind and every moment hurt because you left me behind, It was those times we didn't agree, feeling distorted and totally empty, it was those times you broke my heart and made us feel so far apart, it was those times I couldn't read between the lines, we're all broken up, because it was those times.

I've learned to want better and I've gained self worth, I've learned to be stronger and no longer do I hurt. Because it was those times, my heart knows what's love, knowing love does know me, making peace, happiness and joy my final destiny. Because it was those times, I know where I'm headed and my future is looking bright, holding on to faith and all of what's right.

Because it was those times, I was out of place but now I'm positioned up straight, looking forward and always forsaken hate. Because it was those times, I'm feeling better and my soul has a new design. I'll keep loving, while making love my job to grind, I'm in a better place and the person I was has resigned, I'm now feeling great, because it

Elevation Above Status
"Inspirational poetry" Vol.1

was those times.

Moments Like This You'll Always Miss

A warm touch, hug and a kiss from the ones you love, it's times like these you've always been thinking of. Moms, dads, uncles, aunts, brothers, sisters, daughters, sons and cousins, sharing gifts filled with love while the turkeys in the oven, grandpa's favorite tunes playing on the radio, while the smells of grandma's collards touch your nose. Only moments like this come once a year, although you hope they'll never disappear, you enjoy these moments while they're around, everyone laughing, joking, kids playing with many sounds, as more loved ones are just arriving from out of town. You'll all gather in the living room, listening to what everyone has to say, giving and receiving joy, peace and harmony in every way, feeling like everyday spent on earth was a preparation for today, no other feeling can measure or ever appear to be greater, holding on to the smiles and having family together is major.

Good thoughts and amazing spirits is all that will come

Elevation Above Status
"Inspirational poetry" Vol.1

your way, as your family pray on this Christmas day, there are six nights till the new dawn, this year will be the past and all it had will be gone, yesterday will become old and it will be time to move on, you'll embrace the future and all it brings, loving life with a passion, because of the little things, having memories of the family is a gift in its own, so you pray for those who spent these nights alone, hoping they understand that being alone is still being at home and the best presents you can receive is Jesus presence, a gift of spiritual bliss giving you the glory and joy to reminisce on God's love, the reason for life you cherish, peace on earth should be your only embellish, because it's moments like this you'll always miss.

A Victim Of Wanting To Be Right

Everybody wants to be right, but they are wrong, in any shape, format, structure or form, although your thoughts and feelings should be recognized , saying that it's all one person's fault is nothing but lies. Taking responsibility for your actions should be your major concern and if you don't, you've never inherited the lessons learned, your mind

Elevation Above Status
"Inspirational poetry" Vol.1

is distorted and in that sense is what you speak, leaving your counterparts thoughts or feelings limited and incomplete.

Birds of a feather flock together and whatever you want to do should be the same thing the next person wants too, if they want to go right you wouldn't put up a fight. Who are you to think they are wrong, because they choose to sing a different song. Who are you to say they're not right, because they choose to stay out all night, they're not wrong and they're not right, you are not wrong and you are not right, because in reality you have the option to choose your own fruit ripe.

You want what you want and they need what they need, it goes both ways, but you're choosing to believe what you think you see, needing company, so you spread the word and your audience only repeat what they think was heard, although wrong is wrong and right has yet to be spoken, souls have been tarnished and hearts have been broken, your condemned by your own desire, not seeing through the blur, you don't know how serious things are or what can

Elevation Above Status
"Inspirational poetry" Vol.1

possibly occur. You are responsible for all you go through and no one is to blame for what you do. It's called "to each its own" and if you proclaim to be grown, you would decide to leave negativity alone.

Stop pointing the finger, because you're wrong, stop telling your one sided story, stop praising your actions and taking all the glory, stop feeling guilt free, stop saying it's all about me, stop picking a losing fight, stop being a victim of wanting to be right.

Lifes Journey

Life's Journey: Dungeons and dragons, the Dragons are the demons you'll encounter and the donjons are the places you go on earth. On the journey you walk with the father, taking you into the places, meaning you all the best. Whatever you've done before now is over, but if the past is bothering you and you can't let go, allow your walk with the father to take you pass it and move on, walk on, you might feel as if the world revolves around you, but in all reality, it has nothing to do with you. This mortal experience is nothing

Elevation Above Status
"Inspirational poetry" Vol.1

but an example of who you are. You're going to walk and have a journey with the greatest guide of all.

God, your God, everyone has a God, even if you don't believe in mine. You have a God, your God always talks to you, informing you of what's important. My witness is myself and I can't restrain from the truth, I'm here and I know the tribes and tribulations, knowing my God is here, so with him I walk and the teachings are in the experience. The lessons come from the decisions made, whether it's what you want or not, because it's not about you. Look further than what you look and think bigger than what you think. Some people ask, "why me?" The answer is, "Why not you?" You're just the same as anybody else and in your walk with God you will learn, knowledge is the key to every door and you need to acquire as much as you can on your life's journey.

The Power Of Our Love

Off into the midst of love's abyss, I carry myself by the wings of bliss, my mind is free and my soul's at rest, taking

Elevation Above Status
"Inspirational poetry" Vol.1

me higher into the role I'm blessed. Holding the painting of a life so rare, I see my dreams unfold so clearly, fortunate enough to feel my blessing, no longer alone and no more guessing. The peace is presented in a form so great; a structure so lovely only has me waiting. A touch of beauty in the utmost greatness and there is nothing alive that could ever take this, I'm amongst the gods in ways unknown, feeling at peace I call my home.

Like the wind, I move so soft and smooth, without any thoughts of a world so cruel, it's all here now and the problems are solved and around my fate I will forever revolve. Visions of grace are all I see and lovely faces are revealed to me, this is the place I will always be, the best things in life are totally free. Couldn't even acknowledge moments quite like this, in the past I couldn't Imagine it would ever exist. Everything fits like a hand in a glove, I owe my thanks to God up above, the spirits that hate and wish to break our blood, never can conquer the power of our love.

Elevation Above Status
"Inspirational poetry" Vol.1

Little Things Are The Biggest

Big things come in small packages and it's the little things that matter the most, like opening a door, making a compliment, caressing of the skin, a phone call, a visit, saying thank you, saying I love you, giving advice and like many people say: it's the ...thought that counts. It doesn't take much to give the greatest gift ever, what might not mean much to you can mean the world to someone else... Playing ball with a son or sitting and communicating with a daughter could make all the difference in their life. Going to the store for an elderly person or giving someone less fortunate some materials that you have no use for... Someone's trash is someone else's treasure.

Don't decide to give nothing because you feel as if you can't give enough, because there is no such thing as enough. When it comes to giving, no one can ever get enough of anything, something is always better than nothing. The best things in life are free so this is why they are taken for granted, because people are programmed to

Elevation Above Status
"Inspirational poetry" Vol.1

believe that free is cheap and we all know that something that is free keeps us alive. The next time you think of something to give, don't always think big, and always remember the little things.

My Wife

My wife, everyday I awake I feel good to be alive, knowing you are by my side. There are no words to explain why our love will always remain, through the ups and downs and the good and bad, through the times of joy and the times we are sad. My grace, my peace, my joy, my breath, my life is with you till I have none left. You're the pressure that beats my heart and nothing created could keep us apart. You are my light when it's dark and my sun when it rains; you are my smile when I frown and my joy when there's pain. I thank god for all I've been through, because he was preparing me just for you. I'm built and created to flourish our life, I'm grateful in every way that you're my wife.

Consideration For You

When you're going through anything in life, no one is

Elevation Above Status
"Inspirational poetry" Vol.1

concerned unless it affects them. Your feelings only mean something to people that really love you and yourself; No one else cares. Whatever happens to you will just happen and they will just continue on with Their life as usual, like nothing ever took place. Why should they care? This is the first thing they would ask themselves.

A person should always care because everyone is a subject of the same environment and no one is exempt from life situations, it could easily be them, then they also would feel as if someone else should care. Understanding this would have you take other people into consideration and treat everyone with a sense of concern... Everyone needs someone, whether it's physical, financial or emotional support, feeling the need for comfort is natural for all living and seeing someone in any situation is just like seeing yourself, so why not care?

The power of concern is really healing and would have a long lasting positive effect on many lives. There is no room for being selfish in the world of righteousness, knowing

Elevation Above Status
"Inspirational poetry" Vol.1

you need the same as any other human, also having the exact same senses in life. When you were born you knew nothing and had to be given everything, like learning how to walk, talk, eat, dress yourself and even think appropriately. Everything you achieved was because someone had consideration for you.

Broken Heart

A pain so deep not even a feeling can define the impact. All of the prayers and wishes go unheard and appear as if they were never spoken. Your soul inherits an embedment of torment and malfunctions, thinking about your hopes and wishes. Nothing will save you from yourself and you become your worst enemy. Being strong becomes a way of life, although you bury your true existence within your heart. The truth can't be hidden forever and eventually it will come to the surface. The outcome of your actions will be based upon the length of your emotional oppression. Your life has been driven on the non-acceptance of disappointments and pain distributed to you from others. This defines your present state of mind and your present

Elevation Above Status
"Inspirational poetry" Vol.1

physical condition. At the end of it all you have become what you hate and you've been led to a destination fueled by what you despise, all becoming greater than you, the vital knowledge which should be obtained from your broken heart.

What's A Father

Give praise to the first father, our God, for creating the first image in his name called man, Also a father. This is often forgotten and most times neglected, a man is next in power and given the duties of being a father, protector, guide, director, professor and overseer of all that he possesses. A father stands on his own two feet with the pride of honor, respect and his word. The job of a father starts by becoming a man, making a child not qualify. All men are fathers, by educating, guiding, being responsible and leading by example.

What's A Mother

A real woman has mother tenderizes and a mother's work is never done. In all times of need she's there to count on,

 ***Elevation Above Status***
"Inspirational poetry" Vol.1

loving, caring, nourishing and providing. The credit she deserves always goes unspoken, knowing that every day is mother's day. Women are the most amazing creatures known to man and the power they possess is astronomical. Why not understand their frustrations, coming from the sense of appreciation. Women don't give up, everything you do pays off. A real man loves and respects a real woman, if he doesn't; he's not a real man.

Balancing What's Around You

Be sure to not bring forth regret, because this is a demonistic weapon used to obliterate what has been good to your soul. Know what you're doing when making and molding your future, because the future comes as fast as the next word you read. Balance what's around you, acknowledge and understand what's against you. Stop being a victim of yourself and take advantage of what's good for your health

Change is the most powerfulest reason for new decisions and choices and individuals request change because they become tired, frustrated, aggravated and unhappy.

Elevation Above Status
"Inspirational poetry" Vol.1

Everyone should wonder if the choices they make are correct, because when you change your mind you change your life. Do you love your life?, this is something you should ask yourself.

Most people often get angry with the condition of their life, and because many things appear to be going so wrong, they most of the time never balance them out. The good seems to always be forgotten and the bad seems to always overpower the good, which is more important to you? Be careful of your decisions and make sure your choices have grounds that focus on what is good and means the most to you. This life you live will only happen once and you have control over it all when it's said and done.

I'm Still Here

My atmosphere is good and my emotions are great. It took a long time to come, but it wasn't too late. There are 365 days, but this is the one, my body is getting older, but my spirit's just begun. Every day I awake is a day of birth and every day of birth is a day of work. Headed for celebration,

Elevation Above Status
"Inspirational poetry" Vol.1

it's a time for congratulations, all that recognizes I show my appreciation. Loving what I do and doing what I believe, the love from god is all I need. I'm the reflection of my children because my product's from my seeds; the best in life is free so the best I receive. I look for nothing because everything is always near, my blessings are apparent, because I'm still here..

A quote to grow on by Derrick D Pringle Sr:
"The top is the bottom and the bottom is the top."
"The ending is at the beginning and the beginning is at the end". "Winners never quit and quitters never win."

 *Elevation Above Status*
"Inspirational poetry" Vol.1

Special thanks and dedications to the authors inspirations

(1) God *(Everlasting) The alpha and omega, the true love for all living, the first, the last and the beginning.*

(2) Dr. Martin luther king Jr. *(January 15, 1929 – April 4, 1968) was an American pastor, activist, humanitarian, and leader in the* African-American Civil Rights Movement. *He is best known for his role in the advancement of* civil rights *using nonviolent* civil disobedience *based on his* Christian *beliefs.*

(3) Booker Taliaferro Washington *(April 5, 1856 – November 14, 1915) was an African-American educator, author, orator, and adviser to presidents of the United States. Between 1890 and 1915, Washington was the dominant leader in the African-American community.*

(4) Marcus Mosiah Garvey, Jr., *ONH (17 August 1887 – 10 June 1940). Political leader, publisher, journalist, entrepreneur, and orator who was a staunch proponent of the Black nationalism and Pan-Africanism movements, to which end he founded the Universal Negro Improvement Association and African Communities League (UNIA-ACL). He founded the Black Star Line, part of the Back-to-Africa movement, which promoted the return of the African diaspora to their ancestral lands.*

(5) Malcolm X *(May 19, 1925 – February 21, 1965), born* **Malcolm Little** *and also known as* **El-Hajj Malik El-Shabazz** *(Arabic:* الحاجّ مالك الشباز*), was an* African-American *Muslim minister and a human rights activist. To his admirers he was a courageous advocate for the rights of blacks. He has been called one of the greatest and most influential African Americans*

Elevation Above Status
"Inspirational poetry" Vol.1

in history.

(6) Medgar Wiley Evers (July 2, 1925 – June 12, 1963) was an African-American civil rights activist from Mississippi involved in efforts to overturn segregation at the University of Mississippi. After military service in World War II, he became active in the civil rights movement as field secretary for the NAACP.

(7) John Fitzgerald Kennedy (May 29, 1917 – November 22, 1963),the 35th President of the United States. With help from research assistants and the Library of Congress, Kennedy wrote the book **Profiles in Courage:** a 1957 Pulitzer Prize-winning volume of short biographies describing acts of bravery and integrity by eight United States Senators throughout the Senate's history.

8)**Tupac Amaru Shakur** (June 16, 1971 – September 13, 1996). Shakur's music and philosophy is rooted in many American, African-American, and world entities, including the Black Panther Party, Black nationalism, egalitarianism, and liberty

.